Lost Sherpa of Happiness

Lost Sherpa of Happiness

Poems by

Ken Craft

Kelsay Books

ISBN: 13-978-1-947465-22-0

Kelsay Books
Aldrich Press
www.kelsaybooks.com

For Jill and our bright stars, Lauren and Jeff

Acknowledgments

Some poems originally appeared or are forthcoming, sometimes in earlier versions, in the following publications:

2 Bridges Review: "Piers Plowman" and "Lost Sherpa of Happiness"
Broad River Review: "Here and Gone"
Chronogram: "Into the Urban"
Clover: "Lingonberries" and "Death of a Childhood Friend"
Gray's Sporting Journal: "Hemingway Fishing"
The High Window (UK): "Happiness Bound," "Night of the Dying Frogs," and "Pruning"
Hollins Critic: "Greek Tragedy in a Dumpster"
Kentucky Review: "Parable of the Wren" and "Morning Train"
The MacGuffin: "Reading James Wright"
Pirene's Fountain: "The Age of Narcissism"
Plainsongs: "Sharp-Shinned Hawk and the Song Sparrow"
PoetsArtists: "The Judas Door"
Poppy Road Review: "Self-Portrait"
Roanoke Review: "When Babcia Caught Her Breath" and "Some Hard Talk About Death"
Schuylkill Valley Journal: "Wishes"
Steam Ticket: "Trip, Memory" and "In the Dentist's Killing Fields"
THAT Literary Review: "Window Rain" and "Swim, Camel!"
Third Wednesday: "Jack Writes from Myrtle Beach" and "Waiting for It"
Unbroken Journal: "It's the Fourth of July"
The Well Review (IRL): "Sounding Silence"

Contents

Third Search

About the Author

Deluded people don't realize that their own mind is the Buddha. They keep searching outside.
———Bodhidharma

Obsessed by a fairy tale, we spend our lives searching for a magic door and a lost kingdom of peace.
———Eugene O'Neill

First Search

When Babcia Caught Her Breath

The first summer we owned the camp
we brought my grandmother,
who wore the same one-piece floral bathing suit
each day. I said no, but she took the broom
outside, swatted webs
from the clapboards, tried to reach the eaves.
"Babcia, please! Come. By the water,"
but she bent near the foundation blocks and posts,
pinching and pulling weed heads between rough
peasant fingers, the strong lake breeze
blowing her white hairs, mad dance
of dandelion fluff holding on.
Unbending herself slowly, she swore
in Polish, shuffled to the wood's edge, tossed
ripped roots on Canada Mayflower,
Indian pipe, a Pink Lady's Slipper.
"Come, now," I said. Finally she sat in the Adirondack
beside me, her tanned, bony chest
rising and falling with the sweetness of breath.
Silent, she stared at this lake before her. And me, I inhaled
its strange newness in her name: The waves
against rip-rap. The wild mint smell. The nuthatches
scribing arcs about pine bark.
And, on the water, whitecaps drunk with the passing.
She took this in and more,
then said, simply, "I can't believe
it's almost over."

Some Hard Talk About Death

Such hard-hatted construction workers we are,
mixing abstractions
in that great spinning drum,
pouring concrete talk of our deaths onto the rebar of words,
into the wooden frame of sentences,
aggregate discussion finally giving shape
to the inevitability of our remains.
Yes, decisions are supposed to set and grow firm,
but maybe the temperature or humidity is wrong today.

We agree on fire, at least—the impossible Fahrenheits,
the Christian moksha of ash and bone chip,
but you want us on a hill
in your hometown beside your parents.
Knowing I'll go first, my inner fire begins to flutter,
begins to feel the thinning oxygen
of emigrants strewn across distant ranges
far from the smell of rain and sea,
far from the comfort of soft-bubbling tidal flats.

This is just soot in a box, we're talking, you remind me, returning
the conversation to the set and cure
of a world without our points of view.
But I'm already in a box of cremains,
feeling the pinch of its crevices,
hearing the hollow thumps—the cold weight of Connecticut dirt
dropping from spade-cast skies as I inhale the panic.

No, I say. Better you brace yourself
on a ledge of rock nosing the Sound,
shoes bound by barnacles, wind at your bereft back.
Better you heave me

into a brief black vortex of spinning regret,
my ashes heady with one last westerly, spinning their sweet lies,
settling like gray plankton on the breast of the Atlantic.

Then I can glint like salt confetti beneath the sun.
I can listen as the gulls' calls break up and diffuse. I can release
myself to the cold frontier of wet liberation
while, back on the receding shore, the bright world opens up
like a Winslow Homer: You in a cheerful blue. The whistling box.
Your windblown hair like Shakers in rapture.

Into the Urban

At 10, I liked the horns and the sirens
of Hartford on a Saturday afternoon,
the way roots pushed weedy shoots
between earth-veins of off-kilter sidewalks,
how dimly-lit the long carpeted hallway was,
the creaking of floorboards underfoot
as my mother and I approached
the dusty mahogany door.
Inside my great-grandparents' apartment:
the smell of cabbage, sleepy tick-tocks
of a brass pendulum wall clock,
how Babcia smoked Raleighs
and cheated at cards—only laughing if you caught
her—while a Shirley Temple movie with the sound off
blinked on the black and white TV.
When the adults were busy, I played pirate
on a poop deck at the building's stern, pacing
the overview with its empty wicker basket
and damp bed sheets billowing from the mast
of a clothesline, smelling of city winds and distant ports.
I could lean over the rails, touch the brick walls
of two neighboring apartment houses, pull the cold
iron handle of the garbage chute to peer down
the funk of its black throat. When Dziadek
asked if I wanted to play a game
and all it meant was rolling an empty
Maxwell House coffee tin across the rug
to each other, I said yes despite myself, spellbound
by the strange simplicity. Back and forth,
back and forth, till there was no going back.

In the Dentist's Killing Fields

In the fluoride-free days of the 60s, a boy's
tooth nerves were fair game. The weight of a dentist's
waiting room meant something.

Four beige walls, stoic chairs, pictures
of wildflowers and bees. My feet tiny
clouds over the carpeted ground. I could hear
hunger in the mechanical whine of the dentist's drill:
the room with the white porcelain vortex of water,
the explorers and probes, excavators and extractors.
And, poised above all, the silver praying mantis maneuvering
its spike in and out of a victim's head.
Biting. Spitting. Chewing at its leisure.

The sound sprayed chills across my skin, recalling
past molar trenchings, enamel and bone and saliva popping
effervescence over chin and paper bib.

I tried distracting myself with the shiny-edged page on my lap.
Highlights for Children: the cartoon morality plays,
the black on white antithesis of Goofus inflicted on Gallant.

I tried watching traffic on Center Street; constellations
of cars and trucks and buses rolling to the stop light outside
the office window: pausing, glinting sunlight, accelerating
escapes. Green, yellow, red, green. An old man in fedora, smoking
in his Studebaker; a family laughing in the cavity
of their Impala; a couple stiff as mannequins modeling for Ford.

A woman behind me said, "Kenneth?" nicely, and I glanced
at my father, who refused to look up, flipping his
Field & Stream. The voice led me back to the doctor's.

The meadow of metal. The plastic shell of slippery chair.
The mantis shadows behind an insect eye of light,
tilting and curious about its next mouth.

Last memory: hearing the gurgling, feeling the sucking hook
snag my lip. "Here's a brave young man," Dr. Hebert said, pulling
up his plate of point and pick. "Let's have a look, shall we?"
He donned a mask beneath the fly facets
of his coke-bottle glasses. He leaned heavily into the light.

Escape Plan

"This is us," he'd say, pointing at the boxed red "x"
above our room number, "but if there's a fire, you sure
as hell won't have any red arrows along the hallway
carpet. You'll have that bath towel you just
wrung water out of over your little head. You'll be
on your hands and knees like you just found God.
And you'll have darkness and smoke with screamers
tripping over your body. But you'll be following the way.
The way you're going to memorize right now: left twice
around two corners to the stairwell door. And, if that's
not hotter than a cannon, you'll push it open.
Only then will you stand like a goddamned ghost
under your towel, hold the stair railing if you can, and run
down those stairs like each step's a wrapped gift
of years, because each one brings you closer to this exit"
(his stubby finger finds the bold, diagrammed frame
of a ground-level door), "to the fire trucks and flashing lights,
to the big sound of engines and sirens. Outside'll be the smell
of soot and the glow of fear on all those fire-lit faces
watching this place go up. But that's not important.
You'll be gulping the biggest mouthfuls of smoke-ringed stars
and night-fresh air you've ever swallowed, and you'll be grateful.
Damn grateful, because it's not always the fire, it's the CO2!
Understand? You visualizing good, like I told you?"
And then, like every first hour in every hotel, I took a white
towel, dry for the drill, and draped it over head and back. Like
a fallen angel, wings clipped by dread's shears, I crawled
down the hallway's edge, feeling the clench of my eyes
squint their smoldering embarrassment as other guests
walked by, feeling the hot whites of my father's eyes
watching from behind.

Trip, Memory

It starts with the sound of a whistle.
The smell of cigar smoke
riding bareback on October air.
The cheerleaders' "We got the T-E-AYY-M,"
the dry prayer of their pom-poms.
Me and the boys, uniformly cool—brave
in our home whites and eye black,
our grass-scarred helmets,
our nonfunctional mouthguards,
throwing Hail Mary's and dropping f-bombs,
our bodies bolting
and dangerous with weedy want.

That's all it takes—a somewhere referee's
somehow whistle. I'm 13 again.
I haven't even begun to think about thinking.
The smell of tobacco is a promise,
nothing foreboding.
And the sight of fallen, windblown leaves
rolling toward my cleats is just that
because my veins breathe and bulge as Coach yells
and my blood hits hard to feel the bruise of pleasure
and there's no such thing as symbolism
because death is only something cowboys
and Indians do on black and white TV.

It's the Fourth of July

and he's listening to Oh Say Can You See in a sea of runners and an awakening 8 a.m. heat. The blue smell of Biofreeze on the mentholated old guys & Axe on the sun-venerating young guys & armpit on the just-rolled-out-of-bed lazy guys & no one's run a New Balance step yet. The ellipsis after the song's last line is always a chant of USA! USA! USA! from the fun-run campers who must not read (at least footnotes) because they never feel the wet hand of irony in that disunited "U" running down their body-painted backs.

Jesus, but he bolts when the pistol goes, heat or no. On the course, though, he is passed by sausage-heavy middle-aged men & oxy-huffing retired men & stick-legged kids & women of all stars & stripes. Begrudge not, says the Bible, so he celebrates their speed or their youth, their fat or their fair sex—whatever hare-bodied thing there is to celebrate.

That night, after the picnic-table splinters & charred cheeseburgers, after the fries & bottles of we're-out-of-ketchup, the fireworks mushroom into night clouds & umbrellas rain down hiss & heat sparkle, made-in-China reds, whites, & blues. He cranes his neck, the skies soured with smoke & sulfur, holding tight the hand of his sweetheart.

Then it's blessed be bed, after the *grande* finds its *finale*, only he is wakened by more (USA!) fireworks up the street (USA!) at 11:30 p.m. Still the holiday, after all, ignited by the undoubtedly drunk, after all, because booze is God-Bless-America's drug of choice, after all. The outdoors explodes until midnight & he's had about all he can stand lying down & cursed be Thomas Jefferson anyway, with his noble agrarian society & its whiskey rebellions & its pursuits of happiness & its God-given rights & its who-the-hell-are-you-to-tell-me, question comma rhetorical.

You know how this ends: It's insomnia again. In the shallow, post-patriotic hours of the Fifth of July. Come cock-crow morning, on his walk, Fido sniffs the empty nips & plastic fifths along the sandy shoulder of sleepy roads. There's even a patriotic Bud box, hollowed-be-its-name, white stars emblazoned on the blue of its crumpled carcass.

God bless America, he tells it.

Dream State

The dream is like cough medicine I took as a child,
syrup sweet, where I surface but willingly
submerge anew because the drug grows me gills
for dream water, making me slow, fluid,
pleasant. Mom is young again, for one,
returning from Poland, white luggage, both hands.
Dad has swept and scrubbed the garage floor clean.
Concrete clear of sand, grease, mouse turd,
shining smooth and gray like the day it set. Only
when I lift the garage door, ashen snow stands
six feet high. And my mother, fifty-five years
younger, still wears her Prussian blue coat and pillbox
hat, netting heavy with the heft of blonde hair.
She's waiting for someone—anyone—to welcome
her back. Hug her. Cry out in breathing jags of joy.
Then I wake, unrested. I kill the alarm on the clock
bedside, teach it the protocol of respect, because
my mother has finally arrived.

Heat Vent

On the cold plains of the kitchen hardwood floor.
December, nose to window, glaring in. I dig out
the grilled register near the wall's cool and smooth.
Down that creased ductwork's throat, sawdust,
the orphan screw, a fossilized wasp's last curl.
I sit near the jagged edge, back to the wall,
hum-hypnotized by forced hot air translating
between body and shirt. For five minutes, my spine
interprets the fevers, while below my back,
interlocked wrists dangle down the cell, captive,
thinking: Once, a different house, a smaller body.
When the weight of Siberia bent Connecticut's thin
branch. When I wore cowboy-themed pajamas.
When brief bands of rib could not corral the scope
of my dreams. Grill marks lined the small of my back
branding me one of heat's wild herd.
Now, a man marked by cold and calendars,
I breathe sepia moments in a pensive house,
listen to ticks, soft and metallic. There's the stretch
of skeletal beams and posts and the basement blower,
its patient drone drawing me down. Down to its kind
and forgiving sleep.

Happiness Bound

Sometimes I can smell happiness.
The musk outside my open-windowed
life. I'm anxious. Apollo is bound and gagged in a dark
and orderly back room
where no one's lived (certainly not me) for years.
I swear I can hear it: happiness loping, its graceful
muscles (I imagine) rippling under the sheen
of warm, worn fur (dun-colored).
I feel the urge innate. My claws extend. I get chills
from Truth's hot breath spelunking the ear—
not just pursuit as chase, but pursuit
as takedown, where I can feel the hide,
ride the weight. Yes, happiness!
In its last (not lasting) gallops, alive beneath me,
tripping heavily, the meatiest of thumps
sending clouds of Serengeti into the air of my wishfuls.

But I suspect a Dionysian joke here, hyena
hackles (ha-ha) preening themselves
against the grain of my naiveté. They're yipping
about happiness as pursuit only. Stop.
Not destination. Stop. Or certainly takedown. Stop.
And the message is this: I'm in the open mundane,
not the back room over some golden-locked, dour
autocrat (the lyre), safe life on his sour breath. Stop.
I'm spice in a gamey broth (again) not ground
Serengeti but ground cloves that itch as they climb
the houndstooth of my nostrils in search
of their own starry nights and their own oasis
trees and I wake up.

Still, if I close my eyes again, I can jump—
maybe land—on the back (maybe)
of the myth (maybe). The very thought is deliciously
despotic, is garam dancing with masala.
I want to get weepy with it (happiness, damn you!)
but the paradox ducts are dried gullies already
and that ring slipped off
my thin, cool finger so many years ago already, and I'm just
another man—both Prometheus and bound (not gagged,
alas)—who's been left a Dear John letter (Z). Left
to his just, to his eagle, to his oh-so-dry deserts.

Wishes

"I wish I were never born
because I don't want to die."

Words come easy, but there are realities,
too, like the smell of coffee at 5 a.m.

under the soft butter-light of the oven hood;
the way Antares blinks red and out, red

and out, as night clouds scud by; the Zen
koan of chickadees as they flit

from January to February limb,
white bibs, lemon flanks, relentless cheer

against north-stricken woods. So don't kid me,
wishing you were never born, when you know

your mouth hides zinfandel dreams,
ones where the oak thickens like tannic

moss to the roof of your mouth and your head
releases full lightness to bounce pleasantly

against white ceiling shells, ones where the hands
of Etta James' contralto come up like palms

pressed in prayer. And I suppose when the humidity
gives and the wind turns and a Canadian clipper

sifts the good dry scent of pine through your lungs
like a blessing, it means nothing to you, either.

Worship past and approaching dark all you want, but deny your birthright to this brief, wobbling iridescence?

Lingonberries

I was offering goodbyes
to the 93-year-old mother
of a friend—bedbound Swedish lady,
warm indent of life on pillow, scalp
flaking, regenerating pink skin
under fine filaments of hair.

It was awkward, my farewell,
and her Swedish heritage, her sweetness—
who knows, maybe the red ravines
of her cheeks—reminded me of lingonberries.
As if at some hirsute he-god of Valhalla,
she gazed up, hands pinning comforter
against chin, eyes wide and wary
blue skies. Bone trellises staked
the bruised backs of her hands. Blacks,
blues, purples. Blood betraying from within.

"Next time I visit, I will pick lingonberries
and bring them for you," I said.
"We will make jam for toast." The eyes
changed. No longer seeing me, they seemed to poke
the low-lying thickets of her Swedish past,
searching out these berries. She wanted to place
the word in a bucket—the aluminum bucket of "bush" or "plant,"
"pink" or "red." I wondered if she last
heard "lingonberry" yesterday or 39 years
ago, if resurrecting the word was a kindness or trick.

I never got to hear the satisfying plink of lingonberry
finding the metal well of memory as she recalled it
and whispered, "Ah!" or "Please do!" while lingering

in the small hours of her Scandinavian youth.
I had to leave, and she died a week later.

I think of her now as I open this jar of lingonberry jam
and smell sunrise and fog, mountain laurel and moss.
Butter melting into gentle brown burrs of a Sweden
I never knew.

Window Rain

Sitting at the table near the window
while you visit the ladies' room,
I look out at the rain and recall
college when the drinking age
was 18 and my buddies and I had the stolen
luxury of drinking on weeknights.

We ordered plastic pitchers of beer
at Huskies, topping mugs
before they were empty so no one
could count and no one could brag nine
or nineteen. The more I drank, the more
religion I sensed, both in myself
and in the beer's tiny bronze
bubble chains. No one else noticed.
No one said what the hell.

One night like this it rained
and Glenn started in about this girl
he had taken to his dorm room,
how she said, "My God!" when she saw him
naked. "My God!" he kept repeating
in his cracked-corn girl voice.
We laughed until I noticed the booth
behind us. Six girls. As is true
in all restaurants, you could hear every voice
and none. Between dishes and silverware
and bottles, I figured we were safe.
Still, they had gone quiet when Glenn
invoked his gods.

I wondered what they thought, those girls.
And when, exactly, they got their educations.
The ones their parents paid for
unknowingly. I haven't recalled Glenn
and the girls since that night, really.
But you are still in the ladies' room and, out
on the window, the raindrops are still beading.
They're pausing to think before sliding down the glass.
No one else notices.

Winter Walk

Slant wind and a snow-
seasoned sky with the fine
crackle of ice
reading dead script
off oak trees.
Leaves, rattling
from frozen limbs,
that forgot their
appointed falls.

Once, in Bushnell Park,
I squeezed your hand
to this white pepper sound.
You wore
mittens knit from the early
yarns of marriage
as snow melted
on the soft of your fabric.
I watched flakes
impale themselves on my
palms, crystals scorched
in the branch lightning
of my lifelines.

Scales of Injustice

Glass eye dusty
but dignified,
squatting king
of its squared-tile realm,
the scale mulls weighty
thoughts accumulated
over time—
Milton, maybe.
Heidegger or Kant.

It's all the same
to a scale if you
choose not to gain weight
by not stepping on it.

When you do, though,
watch how uppity
it becomes,
converting Celsius
to Fahrenheit
in hyperbolic fits.
It is fluent
in the language
of natural
causes: Bread-lover's
pizza. OK-one-more-
beers. Rocky Road
ice cream baptized
with warm beanies
of butterscotch.

People wish
to squash it
into submission

as if engaged in battery
bloodsport, but
the black numbers
feint, parry, rise
like Parisians' hands
through gates
at the Bastille.

Insurrections like this
are not quelled
easily. Not when
victorious scales
write the histories.
Not when numbers
dance on the precipice,
defy physics, and
fall up.

The Wife's Weekend Lament

He's reading Simic
in the pantry
instead of trimming
the magnolia,

writing renga
like a ropemaker
instead of weeding
the back garden,

watching Red Sox
work the count
instead of edging
the walkway,

napping on a line
of 2:30 drool
instead of Windexing
storm windows,

but at least he's on top
of the bedspread and
not under the covers,
damn him.

Requiem for an Unwritten Memoir

Cue Mozart. Or Fauré
without his accent *aigu* (now in the *grave*)
because I am about to conduct
choral Lamentations (chapter and verse) re:
my memory, going,
gone-going like talk of royalties
when I lack for a suitably tragic,
memory- and money-inducing hippocampus
with Kafka-esque co-eds and traitorous
family members (e.g. liquor-logged parents who forget to divorce
because they are too busy beating their sons silly).
Perhaps a memoir heavy-eyed with "truthiness," then,
one where my brother and I are found in rain-soggy
bags behind some Stop & Shop dumpster at the rear
of a Jersey (Exit Snake Eyes) strip mall
in Family Year One (a.k.a. "The Struggle Begins").
One where I go to bed each night without gruel,
read *Oliver Twist* under filthy, flashlit bedsheets,
and sneak to the bathroom medicine cabinet
to sniff metallic midnights snapped inside Band-Aid tins
(oh, whiffs of wounds yet dreamed!). One where I muse
on Swiss cheese's negative space—holey as Hoboken back streets
in the heat of August—blessed by horned papal bulls
and swizzle stick-chewing Swiss guards (*taedium vitae*).
One where I snort fat lines of roll-proof Crayola crayons,
flashing the flat sides of their ill-considered,
discontinued "flesh"-colored gravities.

One where I hike outside before dawn onto the call-me-macadam,
is it, or asphalt, was it, while winding through
my family's curbed suburban ghetto of vanilla
and grass, of Briggs & Stratton mower roarings
and Homelite chain-saw whinings.
All in a broken America where cicada buzzes
we have heard on (oval-mouthed soprano) high
reverberate over mailboxes, over red flags raised
to the zip-coded wind. But that's about all I can recall,
coda, because the memoir-inducing memory's so shot (coda)
or anyway suspect (coda)
like Lee Harvey Oswald and John Wilkes Booth (coda
arms), whose suspicious middle names (*adagio molto*)
I uselessly remember, that my agent's gone to lunch,
gone fishing, gone silent and, like everyone else,
given up on every last Godot I've got.

Piers Plowman

Plowman Jake must have flunked
algebra—slope, specifically—or so
it seems as his rusty Ram pick-up
slips down my snow-sniveled driveway.

I watch from my window as the wheels
dial forward & back, braking & sliding,
till I can sniff the burn of rubber
beside the raised brow of my shade.

No salter, no sander, just a truck
bed of snow, Bud-can eyes blinking in & out.
Almost to the top, the Dodge lingers,
spins sideways & slides to the base again.

Jake yanks the steering wheel & floors
the worn pedal of that mothery '04
in a mighty shriek of Goodrich outrage,
sulking ice & buffalo-plaid stink. The tailgate

swings like a madam's ass. He dings the cable
and TV box, giving it an exotic, Pisa bent,
till that old rig clears the summit & jerks
to a halt. Down in jags comes the driver's

window so Jake's gray-stubbled face can
poke out & spit its spiteful f-bomb. Last
I see? Two taillights, gauzy & red. Two open
wounds bleeding in snow & exhaust.

The storm-muffled Ram rattles off. Jake
needs a break, I know. Up the road a piece.
At an unmarked snow monolith erected by
town plowers. Jake, Jack Daniels & a dead end.

43

Pruning

Hours on the back lot, me & a single lopper
against Asiatic bittersweet. Its nihilist vines

wrap the split rail fence, ambush birch & ash,
blanket boulders. Maybe the Audi's next & it's

only April. I think in terms of strategic advantage:
before its bitter sings sweet, before the sun

jazzes its sap, while it's not looking. But it's always
looking. Long slender fingers learning a lopper's

fault lines, finding the hubris inherent in human
marrow, orbiting ankles' smooth vulnerabilities.

Soon the backs of my hands are a history writ red.
Meteoric tales. Raw hands of Ahab drowned

by vine leviathan. Hours on the back lot, me
& a single lopper buying time born to be spent,

slashing the longing, smelling the life infectious.
I can hear it still in the thin hours of night: the hungry

refrain, the rising root of earth's warming choir.

Self-Portrait

There are black bruises on the eggplant
I meant to eat last week,
marring its purple sheen.

On the top shelf of the fridge,
the Tuscan kale wilts, flaccid frills
gracing the glass of good intentions.

The foliage on the treadmill in my bedroom
is muscle shirts draped Dali-esque in
a garden smelling of newness, rubber, seasons.

Along the baseboard, a motley police
line-up: dumbbells, kettlebells, medicine balls.
The faces of guilt.

The Mines Again

Sometimes I wake exhausted with sleep.
Sometimes I need to fall back into dream-
foam shallows, only the Grieg
on the alarm goes *con brio* on me
like a march even if it's a mazurka or concerto.
And next I realize, Christ, only Wednesday.
Sisyphean side of the hump at that.

No one but no one my age should wish
commodities like time away, but king me,
damn it, I'd love to checkers-leap a few hours
to 4 p.m. where I can crawl in a rhombus
of sunlit carpet by the west window, read
12 minutes and nap 43 before supper.
My wife will call from the first
floor's hallowed-be-its-name where the table is set
with cloth napkins, where the black window squares
of the kitchen are pot-roast steamy,
where the polished bird-maple chairs are smooth-slippery
with the rump rubbings of time.

But no.
Instead, it's the boot-camp reveille
of life. It's the slink-off sheet and throw-back
comforter. It's the release of warmth's arms, the bend
into day's breaking bright.
Toward the mines,
damn it, whistling right dwarfish.

The Judas Door

After two days, the taproot of absence spears
this house, nowhere more than the closet
where your perfume and my fear cling
to the fur-lined collar of your coat
against the soft breath of hours.

I fill the hollow inside the kitchen
by cooking and eating summer squash and dill
you planted in the garden last May. I drown
the clock's maddening by sanding and staining new
life into your grandmother's mahogany vanity.

The dog follows me as I move from room to room
and, when I stop, rests but does not sleep,
one cloudy eye half-open and wary.
He's watching that I do not get swallowed,
too. By a door that may not open again.

Death of a Childhood Friend

On the funeral home website, three
color Polaroids, grainy and anemic,
suggest mystery. An Arctic Cat insignia
on his salt-sweat-streaked baseball cap,
askew and cocky, tufts of gray
hanging from the rim. White-stubble tundra
on his flushed, smiling face. An uploaded father-son
portrait, the elder in buffalo plaid shirt
and jeans, the younger's face
half-hidden by upraised beer bottle.

As if adjusting to night, my eyes begin to detect the boy
I knew. Hansel hiding behind the mustache of manhood.
Body still thin. Weathered but sure-footed.
The type death designates as "Remind Me Later."

I read and reread but do not learn.
In the patois of obituaries, once well-knowns do not translate.
Evolved out of sight, a childhood friend becomes Everyman,
born to school, wed, work, bear sons and daughters before
dying like the rest. Missing is the font of clear eyes,
the grass-stained football in young hands,
the smell of outdoor air riding sweatshirt
and dark hair into a house.

"Died at home." The stinginess of how and why
leave my brain begging. I'm the street person
with empty Target bags,
the child caught in adult prison-bones,
cadging charity from nostalgia.

Unconsidered for decades, my childhood friend
was already dead. And me, foolishly,
asking for answers. Trying to revive the neatness of narrative.
Hoping to mourn our shared pasts instead of our shared future.

Skydivers

In radiology, after the doctor
fingers dark pulsars of cancer
on the night of his pancreas,
my friend snaps on
tight goggles of desperation.
Forget the stages.
Forget life's endless
flight. This man will jump.

I pretend to talk like all is
as it was yesterday,
but the tremolo of his jaw hinge
and the similarities
in our salty-eyed shallows
undo me.

Months later, crowding
the foretold day, he flies
through the turbulence of self.
Like any skydiver, he craves
the calmer skies of his wake
as he considers me,
the unreliable comforter,
deep in the fuselage
of my cowardice.

Hesitating but once
before the open door,
he finally leaps
holding hands with the dignity
of his silence.

I should crawl,
find his speck as it plumbs
its airy depths.

Instead, I hide,
watch wind whistle
in its rivet-framed hole of sky.

Second Search

Sharp-Shinned Hawk & the Song Sparrow

All spring, the punctured sky collapses blue
beneath the shrill knives of their call.
All day, shriek and talon, eye and hunger
from the heat of a red-black gullet.

They circle overhead, dive under liquid
evergreen, glide through currents of hardwood,
trunk and limb. Nestling, fledgling,
songbird—on ground or mid-flight—
leaving only an orphan feather for changeling.

And here I hear the song sparrow sing.
Here in the narrow interstice between stealth and wait.
Her three notes. Her cheerful trill. Her hesitation
at the wood's held breath.
Then, song again.
To sun or cloud, maybe. Wind or mate.

She sings to the stillness of quiet's dull edge.
She sings to not knowing that every joy
in life is answered, eventually.

Parable of the Wren

It's when I'm feeling small,
silenced by the din
of black dogs

that I consider the wren,
how she bursts from the brush
of stick and contrast, perches brazen

on the deck's railing cap railing regally.
Mere child's fist-fluff, this dowdy
drop of feather and cocked tail

flaunts her joyful gall and outsized song,
deciding where to nest next—the warp
of my dark or the weft of my design.

Possum

One morning a possum, dead on a wooded
edge of sidewalk. No blood or wound. Fur
white & wasp-hive gray. Lush & winter-healthy
in the spring sunlight. I expected the town to shovel
rigor & mortis, but next morning the dog & I found

her waiting again, eyeless now, eviscerated
by the beaks of night. In a week there was less still
& she moved. Pawn-slide. Sleep chessman's opening play.
Today, weeks later, she reproaches the living with three
latitudinal ribs, broken prison bars of her possum soul.

Desiccation curls her possum sneer. A single incisor tears
eternity from the air. Only the bone-colored tail grows
stronger. Leathery. Immortal. A parenthetic permanence
off the path. On the way home, I look up and see the bend
of a contrail. What's left behind: a cold longing in the sky.

The Snake Aquatic

I really wish she
had never seen that snake
sunning itself
on the rip-rap only to come and find
its clay-colored tats
more safely ensconced
in the glossy graphics
of my *Reptiles & Amphibians* guidebook,
where it basks as a Northern Water Snake
harmlessly stretching
its four patterned feet
against the dark
tropes of my instincts.

Now I'm loath to dive
into this cold-blooded lake,
because the snake "will flee
if given the chance,
but flattens body and strikes
repeatedly if cornered," and I know
how it feels to be cornered
repeatedly,

which gets me to thinking repeatedly
how water snakes
are cursive narratives floating
their rising suspense.

The D'Nealian swoops and curves.
The sudden loops and slashes
that make them the story's climax writ large:

snakes as ropes of wet adrenaline, snakes
as keeled scales
on taut cables of tension, heads held high
out of water,
accenting the diacritic fangs of fear.

Swim, Camel!

What's night but a long wait
to unlock the foil coffee
bag, take a sniff, and listen to the crackle
of grinding beans? Why count sheep when you
can recite mantras to the clean stream
of boiled water—that silver string from kettle
to mug—the steam and soft baby-bubble steep
of wet grounds easing into a filter?
It's the day's gift to me, the Sumatra smell,
the earthy taste of coffee rising on the tongue.
Second and third reassure, but it's the first
that marries you to morning.
Trouble is, molding ritual
from coffee makes a man
late, rushes you,
forces you to take a cardboard circus
of animal crackers to the bathroom
and breakfast there
as the shower heats. Sweet hissing.
Steam again. Naked
with a cupped hand of cookies. Plunging
in. You'd think you could keep
a prayer secret from the showerhead's
prying eyes—and I admit the cookies
stay dry and crunchy
at first—but somehow the giraffe's neck
darkens and swallows
itself soft before I can eat it.
And the elephant's next. Its trunk drops
off and inches for the drain
before I can trumpet the alarm.
That leaves the camel—

or is it dromedary? Hell with it.
I just open my hands and make of its hump
an offering. One camel sidestroking
in circles, in its private oasis yet.
That'll be me in the office cubicle an hour
from now as I do the brainless mechanical again.
Me. The beast of burden
dissolving in style, counterclockwise.

From the Unwanted Dog-Poem Pound

Already flushed from bed by his wife's restless legs & their ascent up the loose scree of nothingness, Tony sleeps on the couch again. Soon he's scratched from the subconscious state of Connecticut thanks to the damned *dog noir* on the floor, its back paw threshing its ear & the concomitant tingling license with its jingling rabies tag & Jesus, dog, will you be quiet, he says, & it will—out of curiosity for the mysteries & gifts of the human voice—but darkness & boredom conspire to return it to its toiletries & by God, he's going to kill the dog if it doesn't stop littering sound all over this clean sward of silence.

He does not have to see to detect that the dog's lips are now curled with its stained Chiclets bared as it works its hairy haunch like a black cob of kernel corn back & forth, back & forth, like a typewriter carriage returned from the Lazarus dead.

"Stop!" & he's blessed briefly & dozily with relief sweet & slow as blackstrap molasses when his dog wets the stillness by licking its plumbing under cover of living room night, over & over, playing the dog's ace of spades, tongue & groove, happy & entitled like a casual rogue rolled against the wall of this un-kenneled purgatory.

Man's best friend, my ass, he figures, so he pitches a pillow into the night's yelp & the case is finally cracked as the dog retreats to the kitchen, clunks bonily to the floor, & lets loose its "can't-live-without-'em" sigh of bruised dog pride.

Night of the Dying Frogs

Raining. Restlessness.
Wet streets & the wan smell
of drowning earthworms.
The deluge-drummed hood
on the drive to work before dawn.

Ahead, halogen slivers of silver
pin effervescent puddles
in sibilant streets.
Sound of water-hosed wheel wells.
Smell of amphibian air creeping the car's
phosphorescent cave as headlights
pith the darkness.

Then, to a Biblical beat, rain-bloated
bullfrogs in the road. Their fat, refugee leaps.
Crossing. Fleeing.
Right to left.
Pond to perdition.

I swerve between slicks of them,
jumping sacks
of green saturation, golden-eyed
with apocalypse as if pursued
by Aesopian stork gods
stilting about the woods or a French chef
sheathed in the bog & whetstone of night.

My tires speak the quality of mercy,
slurring soliloquys beneath wet brakes
as these dark croaks of life, yellow & green, live
& die with only the briefest of benedictions,
only the reddest of blessings
in tail-lit exhaust.

Puddle Duck at Picking Time

Knee deep in lake,
picking blueberries
from an overhanging
highbush, I hear
a gentle ripple
near my leg.

It's a female mallard
come to scoop-sip
floating berries that miss
my colander, come
without fear, too,
having been fed bread,
no doubt, by renters
and vacationers up shore.

A basic camp tenet
obeyed since childhood:
Never feed ducks!
Ducks who chuckle-
quack. Ducks who
flock like rock groupies
and hangers-on. Ducks
who shit cloudbursts
underwater—parasitic
poofs, a doctor
will tell you, raining
duck itch upon
swimmers like you
and me.

So polite, though.
So patient and demure
in her duckish way.
Never once biting
my thigh with impatience
or impertinence.
Never once demanding
my attention
like some squirmy kid
in a grocery store's
cookie aisle.

Rather nun-like, too,
in her stoic faith
and vow of silence.
Her mottled brown
and buff habit,
her Cheetos-glow
bill and rubbery feet
working the water
in yellow-orange strokes.
An industrious duck.
A humble duck.
An if-Emily-Dickinson-were-
reincarnated-as-laconic-duck
duck.

Not that you asked,
but the sound
of every tenth blueberry
dropping into lake
goes like so:

Ker-plink.

Variations on a Theme of Feathers

1.
Nests: Downy hollows,
warm mud and twigs, mouths
like miters of minor bishops.

2.
Once, a crow's pinion
riding the door crease
of a white Volkswagen.

3.
After the seagulls:
the sandy cartridge and plume,
the cracked shell.

4.
Before foam.
Before TempurPedic. Gooseloads
in protean pillows.

5.
Under the bird feeder
and after the cat: yellow tape, notepads,
police cruiser strobes.

6.
Once upon a lady's hat,
alive and buoyant.
Flight decks of fancy ever after.

7.
On the sliding-door glass,
feather-bruised bullseye
over a broken body.

Another Calling

A moth, heavy
with water-
wounded
wings, fluttering
on the lake
as if the surface
were hot.

It sends
circular sonar,
saintly halos
of life
to the distant
bass of its
deliverance.

Greek Tragedy in a Dumpster

Heat of July. The close air of the Maine woods close behind a grade school. Playground, still ghostly with the shrill silence of absent children. The usual quiet after my run is disturbed before I get in my car—thumps in the dumpster out back.

I steel myself for garbage with heart and find an adolescent raccoon staring back. Black mask doing solitary. Marble eyes of night with their tiny apertures of light. His bristly fur heaves in low, oatmeal-black breaths. A shallow history of what befalls hunger.

Perhaps he is confused by his first human, perhaps by daylight—this midnight unmasked—so foreign to his forays. Four torn McDonald's bags lie around him, but the regal Tudor-king remains are long digested. Royalty has given him the slip, and life is a stubborn throne of gravity—Sisyphean, if his sliding knew. Sartre would sympathize, too. No exit. Hell as others' leftovers in a bunker of hard and smooth.

I find a rotting 8-foot beam, once the smart wooden edge to a now-unfunded school garden, slide it over the dumpster's lip and down its metal mouth. The raccoon retreats.

"Deus ex machina," I assure it as I leave.

Original Sin

Last time Adam left the garage door open, he braked the Ford as a snake slid in, a shiny rope of coal massaged in mica, long as an island on July's wobbly horizon. The serpent lost itself in tenements of aluminum trashcans, spider-webbed milk crates, four-year-old bags of fertilizer, and cheap plastic shelves stocked with paint, 3-cycle oil, and terra cotta clay pots.

Stepping out of the car, he sensed how space shifts when slick with silence and snake. The humble square of concrete and air was no longer homey, for one thing. Not like the one stinking of Friday's buffalo chicken, 5-month-old beer bottle empties, and spilled gasoline.

Lord. That eve his wife laid down the law: Pick this garage clean, like bones from filet of flounder. Today! But he hesitated. His birthright clearly stated: Thou shalt not be buried with the adjective "snakebit" tattooed into thy skin. He went duck, duck, gooseflesh just thinking about those twin pricks of pain!

So he reopened the garage door, backed the car out. That, and with his only begotten son raising cain at a friend's, placed the boy's gerbil, Knowledge, in an opened Budweiser box on the driveway. The sound of tiny claws on shiny cardboard as he snuck inside to play sentry at the living room window was like lint on the sweater of his conscience.

When the snake slipped its garden, all coil and tongue and intestines of desire, Adam clicked the garage door remote, listened to the hum-homilies of motor, pulley and chain, and murmured, "Forgive me, Father, for I have sinned. Again."

Later, he ventured to the pet store to replace Knowledge with Ignorance. In cages thick with the smell of life's wood chips, they mix easily.

Third Search

Reading James Wright

I have been wandering with Wright
These two hours, under trees
Shadowy with women and dance. Soon it is dusk.
Somewhere horses
Move. The flint of hooves. The stone masking soft
Kindnesses.
He doesn't know I am here, mistakes
Me for loneliness on a sturdy branch.
I leave him to his
Beautiful dark,
The dampness of give beneath my feet.

Hemingway Fishing

Chased to Idaho by fame and paranoia,
Hemingway sips the slow intoxications.
He dreams first and always
the unheated flat, wife Hadley
breathing contrapuntal cold
with boy Bumby. The cat, F. Puss,
watching Hemingway's shadow
creased and swallowed by the door.

In the dream, it is Paris again. Hunger again.
Bone of discipline and puddles
between cobblestones.
Smoke over mansards. Coffee. The warmth
of café braziers and whispered French.

And in the writer's dream, Michigan.
Fox River and the current of youth's flow.
Its lovely lies. A knife-sharpened pencil scratching
Moleskine lines so the water can branch
and eddy and brood over a deep hole
where cedar and birch scatter shade.

On the surface of the pool, a trout halo
radiates until its curves
reach the river's heart where Hemingway,
in his father's waders, stands.
Here the sound of line and impaled grasshopper,
mouth spitting up hook and death,
lash the air. Here Hemingway's legs,
fully submerged, begin to feel
a cold grip and the first leaden pull
of Idaho downstream.

Morning Train

Outside before the day
breaks with joy, the first sound I hear:
dark whistle of the Ashland train.

It speaks of paths
overgrown, people stepped past,
dreams diagnosed as sleep.

The fading climbs inside me, curls
a last bend, settles soft in memory's slow.

I walk on without it, with it within,
my ribs its worn tracks, my heart its worn rumble.

Elements of Yellow

include echoes
from grade-school hallways

daffodil-
buttered snow from below

and not caring—
softly.

Also the past shucked
of misery's husk and tassel:

nostalgia's bright
hindsight sniffing
candy-tin darkness,
empty canary cages seeking
fugitive songs,
6-year-old hands
rolling saffron orbs
from Play-Doh still warm
with the whiff
of immortality.

Don't forget yellow's
adaptation and evolution.
Like the seeds
"what" and "if"
dreaming in lemon,

or the wobbling copper
cast of first sunlight casing
hemlock bark,

or the forearm grip
of adolescent gold on
imagination's greed.

And yes, the shyness
blowing across fields of mustard.

Here and Gone

excluding a war zone
human death remains
the mad relative
hidden from sight
while nature
files and catalogues
its dead on the public
narrative of roads

why then
looking down on these shallows
at this same school of minnows
hanging in the same green-peg balance
as last month;

looking at
this same dragonfly
stutter-flying the water's stippled surface
as last summer;

looking at
these three smallmouth bass
swimming over the same soul shadows
against gold-gilled sand
as ten years ago;

am I reminded of you

and why would this moment
choose me to endure the eternity
inherent in minnows, dragonflies,
and soul shadows

Neighbors

First snow and Mrs. Cahill's adult child
in his navy parka rushes the kids
who scatter to houses like juncos
when a blue jay explodes
onto the feeder. Look at him:
Indian maize teeth, ungloved
marbled-red hands, wind-teared,
weathered cheeks.

He's seen dogs leap and heard children
shout. Limbs energized by their laughter, maybe,
or by the geography of his own distant youth,
perhaps—a foreign
country with snow-bunting along split rail fences,
small yards stitched together so memory's pattern
can't get lost. He can't possibly know
how to roll snowmen from cold neglect,
how to pack them in three icy globes.

He's swiping off his hood now, uncorking coils
of salt-and-pepper Slinky. To a sky gray
with falling snow he makes his offering: unshaven face,
pink calf-tongue, eyes clenched with wrinkled wish.

Then he extends his arms,
flops hard on his back, blades
Snow Gabriels onto the lawn.
A new Vitruvian soul —square of solitude,
circle of snow.

From behind the windows
meanwhile, parents and neighbors

handicapped only by consternation and frowns.
Cellphones hitting "record." Thumbs
texting something-should-be-done. Heads
shaking from the hollow kilns
of intolerance.

Unplanned Poem

You can't write a poem without a plan.
So you execute: Walk the dog, set inspiration's stanzas

while he sniffs shrubs brushed by rabbit haunch,
tracks snow crust caved by deer hooves, licks lemon

Lascaux pissed hollow by other dogs. Only it's 4 below
before dawn, and you're distracted by a certain polar intimacy

with your lungs, by the idea of long underwear left
hanging over the bedroom chair, by the part of you

that's dying melodramatically as white helixes
twist in the air's brittle being—breath rising to

a bottomless sky only to be consumed by the cold logic
of universe and stars, of Einstein and God.

The Body Hides

its prison bars
but cannot hide screaming
inmate thoughts within.

God, Philosopher-Warden,
counsels the graying hairs:
Don't heed
"the best years are behind you"
whispering warm
in your Orpheus right ear,
tickling warm
in your Lot's wife left ear.

And please, don't feel
any parental obligation
to stare at the rusting
swing set out back,
the way a lonely wind
kicks its feet too high,
moving it,

moving the empty seat
in you.

Tempus Fugit

Hour glass chambers
wide as August heat
chafe days cricket-deep
in humid thought.

Human eyes blink
at the wasp waist,
gauge the fleet
softness of its sand needles—
thin threads of the past
stitching down our feral futures.

The chamber above exhales
the airy years.

And below,
the vernacular of flow.

The Speed of Apocalypse

Einstein taught that light
has no equal but the speed
of gravity.

Convenient for learned astronomers
who sip calculations and tonic
for fun

assuring us
we have but a few ticks past 8 minutes
to finish our tans

and orbits
once God changes His mind
about the sun.

Idyll Thoughts

I lift my eyes from Jack Gilbert's words, "All the ways
of growing old," my body rocking to the pleasant
rumble of tracks and train. Sixty years sliding
by the window, but it's not my past streaming
along Connecticut shoreline. Instead, small cottages
with clapboards salted gray, glowing with inhaled light.
Me on the front step: white-haired, wrinkled, worn
from a short run, maybe, skin sweat drying to tanned tackiness.
Healthy, even breaths, early summer tracing
the softening hoop of ribs. That's me, all right,
conjugated in the future perfect. Years after today's
sunlight blinking through June's trees and Amtrak's
window onto Gilbert's line: "Surely our long, steady
dying brings us to a state of grace." I know because it's
morning and the cottage walk has a curl of smoke-furred cat.
I know because I don't even like cats. Yet. And the imagined
drowsy smells: cut-grass dew. Bruised lemon balm.
Ocean. And the garden coursing the tributaries of my palms.
And fingers with earth that won't embrace me with its dark love
because sickness and pain don't live on the Sound
I'm passing. No. Trapped inside this double-paned train
window, they can only yearn for years been, might-have-been,
to be. How do I know this? I hear the horn of others'
misfortune as we hurtle by the marsh at low-tide, that's how.

Passenger Seat, Route 1A

My God, the boxes:
the trailers and the double-wides,
the ranches and the shacks,
the sheet-clotted windows, open
doors gagging up
one-armed dolls
and stained
blankets pregnant with rain
and mildew. Post-apocalyptic
lawn mowers
abandoned mid-swath
lean against berms of tall grass
thick with the thrum of crickets
and August.
But the boxes most of all!
The pennants at the ends
of their dirt driveways
proclaiming cottage industries:
OPEN flags, once-colorful,
once waving, now limp and anemic
with sun and years.
The hand-painted signs
spelling Wild Maine Blueberries
or Tourmaline Here or Camp Firewood $5
in crooked letters.
And I think, with my brow
against air-conditioned glass,
My God, can they get out?
Can they escape? Are they happy?
It's only when we hit
the pothole and I bump
my forehead that I remember
the moving box I am in.
My God.

Waiting for It

Her veins are too small and brittle,
the nurse says, rolling the IV away
so I'll know the end has finally
found its beginning. I sit on the edge
of the bed each day anyway,
pressing the cool softs of her hand
as if I can will warmth
into the chill of her being. My grip,
failsafe as winch and rope,
hauls and holds her up. I don't
want her to be alone in that dark
place behind those closed eyes.

Sometimes she scares
me, raises her arms above
her head in a slow thrash,
as if a nimbus of bees
has beset her. Then the rapid
breaths, like she is running
and stopping as morning passes
through day's shadow.

The nurse whispers *it won't be long now*.
It sounds like *I told you so*. It sounds
like *who do you think you are?*

When she leaves, I lean in and speak
in the wrinkled well of ear,
down the hollow of its secrets.
Hang on, conspiratorially.
I'm here beside you.

She shakes her head no
once. Mama says when it's time,
she'll want it, that help and delay
are ignorance and cruelties.

But I do not and will not believe.
I deny. I deny.

Walking on Water

God knows I'm no Christ figure,
but I would like to walk on water
just to pour the sensation
from my bucket list. One day, on a lake,
my feet dry and cool, skating
the wet roof of morning, sun shards
scintillating under heel. Another day,
August afternoon, West Indies:
turquoise dust silky as silt softening
my toes, ten warm psalms in salt.

Then, on an Atlantic night,
phosphorescence making lanterns
of my legs so they blink
lighthouse-like. (Behold the holy
mackerel rising—open-mouthed, amen
tongues out, panes of their sideway eyes
surfacing like curious glass to the glow!)

I fear only God and doubt.
Covenants and dictums.
The cancer hiding in will
as one wanders His seven seas.

But, courage! Even failure holds
consolation: the fathoms' cold,
the camaraderie of sailors' bones,
the last act of contrition that comes
with looking up in the name of
the bubbles, the glare, and the holy shadow
that was my faith.

The Age of Narcissism

I read it in *The New York Times*:
We live in the Age of Narcissism.
To commemorate, *Bon Appetit* issues
its "culture" issue.
Nothing to do with Ancient Greece
or the Renaissance. Nothing to do
with the tang of sourdough starter
or tentacles of kombucha mothers.
People, rather. Photographing
their food before they eat it. Because
if it isn't uploaded
and shared, they didn't eat it.

From memory's rib, photography.
And after dessert, selfies. Where diners
hold the Palm God high, stare down his shallow
pool, sacrifice bulging eye-white, toothed hyperbole,
melon-slice smile.
Homily of click.
Benediction of send.

Check back for likes.
And more moments later. These are the new
immutables: the kiss of reaffirmation
and cold food.

Jack Writes from Myrtle Beach

Just sitting behind my Wayfarers here, watching
one fine girl-woman—you know the type!—
with some lucky-ass pretty boy,
the two of them among us
but not.

They're on this low rock wall by the jetty now,
her halter top a hammock of happy
and her cut-offs cutting at the last
possible moment. Long hair, sun-
drowning brown to bleach,
freckles across the nose and cheeks,
all why like Cassiopeia in the sky (look it up, loser).
Between her lips, just enough tooth
to suggest, like she's hiding some secret
and holding back just to show she can.

The dude turns his back to the beach. His size-14
heels hang off the rock-hard wall and his muscle-hards
tense as her hand hides that suggestion of tooth, giving
off a little suspense and a little sexy. One, two, spring-
coil three! Backward flip and over he goes,
like the big show planting his big
bares in this hot land of youth-worshipping sand.
(I felt old just watching, for chrissakes.)

Does she shriek? Does she applaud? Not hardly.
Just slides her tan fingers through the curtain of curl
at the back of his neck as they walk off
with the indifference of beautiful people parting
the plankton of fat and old and ugly
floating above the high-tide mark.

Wish you were here…

Adam & Eve Asleep on Old Orchard Beach

They look too perfect, this young
couple gleaming on towels in the sand,
each freshly-kilned, each glazed by a God
nostalgic for first days—garden days of
lions and lambs, of fertility
and fig trees.

See the rise of her breast, the fall of her belly:
mathematic measures of the sexual tenses. Beside her,
a swollen *Cosmopolitan*, sea breeze lazily leafing
models' knowledge-crazed hair
and overripe lips.

And him: all line and shadow,
muscles and bones straining. Like June-struck earth,
the green urge, the lying in wait.

God forbid they open their eyes now.
They'd rise and look down on our wonder.
They'd bite words from the tart white air
and talk, tongues confirming the worst.

Taps

"Colleges known as the Seven
Sisters?" she says.
"Let's look that up."
And her thumbs *pas-de-deux*
on the ice rink of her phone's glass.
Taps, I hear. Her thumbs
peck like hens for feed
and the reflection of cold data
slides off the polish
of her nails. "The three
you were missing are Barnard,
Bryn Mawr, and Radcliffe,
which was integrated into Harvard
for good in 1999." She continues
to read but her voice breaks up
and fades. I've already wandered
into the dry arroyos of incomplete
lists because me, I'll take the wonder.
Or the slow suspense of unwinding
the wonder. So for now there remain
but Three Horsemen of the Apocalypse:
War, Famine, and Death; four
deadly sins: pride, greed, lust, and envy;
and two magi, robes smelling
of camel and the scorch of sand:
Melchior with his frankincense,
Gaspar and his gold. And the last?
He's packing dates and wonder
as he approaches the manger.

From a Dock on a Maine Lake

Lying here, side of my head resting
on the crook of right arm and gazing
from the grotto of my right eye,
I hear the water and see the creased
dam of my left elbow, the occasional bird
flying through its wild blond grasslands.

The left eye, though. It peers over
the tanned levee, sees the high gold-shot
lake—so high it threatens
to flood and marl the east shore
where clear sky, punctured by treeline,
seeps anemic blue to airy bone.

Shifting to my back I get the sky's
gas-flame blue scribed by pine and maple
treetops, the firmament a forgotten
language from first-person point of boyhood.

And the wind! The needles and leaves
nodding like anxious ponies,
wagging like old ladies' heads
at green gossip. Trees exhaling a ropey
poem of clouds. White thoughts, broken
words, startled birds put to flight. They flock,
elongate, twist and split open like smoky time
seeking its own shore to roost.

Sound and Fury

From upwind,
boats on the water
make no sound.
This is how life
in review might appear:
the marriage
of speed and silence,
the doomed momentum,
the noise pursued and
taken down by distance.

The fiberglass flashes.
The boats' windows
glint. And, somewhere,
a sun wheels. The eye,
though, is drawn
to the thrill of waves,
the chop and fan of water,
the cannibalizing foam.

From the boats' vinyl seats,
the motors must be
impressive, all din
and conquering confidence.
But from shore,
the boats look
like memories
dragging the heaviness
of their wakes:
white lifelines seeking
neatly branched ends
on the palm
of a morning lake.

Sounding Silence

You ask for a definition of silence,
but there's too much noise
in the denotation of dictionaries.

And no, I won't bemoan technological
flies hectoring the flesh of our days,
but instead take you at your word,

since you gave it to me. Like a scientist,
I'll coax silence into the open,
bait it with white-coat logic.

By unplugging the house. By shutting my eyes.
But silent antonyms, like mice, flatten
themselves. They creep through cracks

with whiskered ease until I feel
the tickly brush of wooden beams creaking
and the glancing sniff of wind at the windows

wondering about me, pressing the framed
glass, muntin and sash. Conclusion: Even
with wax plugs pooling my ears,

silence fails me. It mocks, tracing circles
round the ringing until the resonance
of tinnitus combs the fine hairs of my cochlea.

So I'll assume my own definitions—the "isn'ts"
that make silence what it is.
Summer mornings, maybe. The cicada's

drawn, declining cry. How it celebrates a sort
of silence once it stops. Or autumn afternoons.
The un-silent silver of airplanes' slippery flight,

their engines cupped beneath hollow domes of sky,
their contrails breaking where white cries loneliest
for blue. Will that do in lieu of silence?

Dream Where Pain Escapes

In the dream,
pain leaves her one rib
hanging—
cracked white wicket
and the sweet whistle
of remembrance.

She walks unfettered
and the world is
underwater moss,
the almost of silence
beneath clouds
of burnt milk.

The sky enters her,
exploring the wonders
of her wound. She inhales
the tickle of thoughtless
life—the only true life.

Soon the damp
fur of distant woodsmoke
and pine, dead leaves
and mud, climb her nostrils.

And in the forest, prints
deep and perfect. She kneels,
fingers the tracks'
hollows, smells
fugitive musk,
lifts the flake
of dried iron to her lips.

When the sky finally rains
its opulence
on her hair and cheekbones,
the oval of her mouth
sings pain's stolen howl.

There's no echo or reply.
Only the airy song of sky.

An Old Man Walking Dawn's Borders

Before dawn, when the sky
dreams its Delft moments,

treetops cast black maps,
a celestial cartography with cays

and peninsulas and bays
of uncharted shoreline.

That's the time he walks
his child mind.

It sees adventures in outlines
on the road, shadows

left by night creatures,
the fresh past of flight

still hanging like the smell of rain
in the heavy air. He sees soft oranges

and yellows framed by windows
in strangers' houses, squares lit

like pulsing coals still
mulling last night's

kindling and flame. He
blesses each home

with a grandmother
and wicker sewing basket,

the smell of wax
in a child's coloring book,

lightning creases in
Father's leather chair,

ghost prints of flour
on Mother's apron fabric.

The carpentry of memory:
these houses are populated

yet empty, their glowing
insides like butter melting

in the airy bellies of biscuits.
Lord forgive him

such domestic idylls.
He should know better.

Which is why he walks
his child mind

when the sky can only
dream its Delft moments,

when dawn is still an explorer
anchored off tree-scoured shores.

Last August E-Mail

The day after company leaves I wake to rain
at 4:30. Your nightgown floats through rooms
to close windows and dry the floors.

I get separated from sleep
and can no longer dream it.
The still house, so recently resonating

with voices, has grown loud in its silence.
A haunting thing, especially the bedroom
my parents slept in. Its emptiness

damn near swallowed me while I vacuumed last
night, as if my parents were gone for good
instead of only driving south through nine circles

of Beltway. But now it's just another Maine
morning, window screens heavy with mercury prayer
beads, lake in its metallic mood as you sleep.

So, yes, I should be writing poetry, not staring
out windows, but the summer's withered to a weekend
and life despises the numbering of days

because numbers, like words, are
unforgiving things and there's a single
red maple leaf curled and clinging

wet to the window. There, just above the sun shining
on these cool, gray floorboards. There, where those
coins of rain you forgot reflect an early fall.

Evidence of Work

Only now, idle enough
to feel rips and tears
in the fabric of flesh,
do I see the wounds
of yesterday's yard work—
itchy pinhole of red
blushing atop the hard
roof of my left foot.
L-shaped laceration
angling under a torn
flap of cotton jean
against my thigh
and, on my right ring finger,
a pink-rimmed scallop,
one small divot of ache
under an eyelid
of expired skin.

Evidence of work,
of the beautiful numbness in
purpose and movement.

As to how's sharp cut
and when's quick puncture,
work will not speak. We closed
camp in Maine, is all I know
or need to know: October
day, cloak of rain,
leaves pinned to earth
like black-burdened butterflies.
That, a sodden fog
spun in the cold spindle of trees,

and me working
from under the broody weight
of thought.

School for Sleep

Today his brain fights against the slag of fatigue.
He attempts naps, but the neighbor's Dalmatian barks off sleep's
white noise just as he reaches the black moment.
Then the phone rings
for long-lost hooks, and a sweaty solicitor
with clipboard and backpack presses
the dirty doorbell of *dormez-vous.* Twice.

He cannot find sleep's border,
the hay smell of its cut fields under August moons,
the closed-eyed cat stretch
of its warm, dust-beamed barn dream.

The insomniac body and mind,
shadow dancing with dementia—it's coming
for him, furtive as Birnam Wood.

Some dawn soon, after the incoherence
of a million cricket nights, after
his sagging body has been ferried by an exhausted wife,
dragged and left in the honey-cells of assisted-living,
he will be bathed, toweled dry, and fed coloring-book meds
until he forgets his rich harvest
of milestones and conformities—graduation, marriage,
children. Some dawn soon, his mouth will cry out
for a mother and father many decades dead,
a final humiliation.

Like a comet hiding its dust, ice, and guilt,
his wife will bring her brightened conscience
to view his still-here each day.
And, swaddled in industrial white, his mortal coil

will sleep at last. Through entire visits. To the mantra
of bee-glade voices, stinging the ears sweetly
with, "Such a sunny day outside!"
"Isn't it beautiful? Wake up and look, Dear,
wake up!"

Lost Sherpa of Happiness

Some days, when my nostrils
are reedy with the scent of pine needle and frost,
when the sky is a sun-fused thing reigning
blues, I thank my Sherpa of Happiness,
his yellow coat ahead, and let the dry swish
of tall grass against his canvassed thighs
suffice as reply.

Mine is an unthinking gratitude.
I've seen how thoughts can deflate
the wind and douse the sun in a wheel of fog.
I've seen snow, mountains, and regret
heap the horizon as my Sherpa guides me
past you-should-know,
stepping over question-this,
and taking long shortcuts around what-about-that.
I learn by example. His conscience—
noble and savage—thrives in being lost
and disbelieving it. His simple clothes,
unwashed, wrinkled by a rootless past,
smell of earth, moss, cold air
in the pockets.

Like his forebears, he plants his staff
and reaps his strides in the innocence
of this brightness. Now and again I hear laughter.
Not a joke he recalls. Simply the stroke of luck
that has chosen him, here and now,
to lead me toward dusk and doubt,
to walk me through this tenuous moment
of wilderness.

About the Author

Ken Craft is a teacher and writer living west of Boston. His poems have appeared in *The Writer's Almanac, Verse Daily, Plainsong, Gray's Sporting Journal, The MacGuffin, Off the Coast, Spillway, Slant* and numerous other journals and e-zines. *Lost Sherpa of Happiness* is his second poetry collection. His first, *The Indifferent World*, appeared in 2016. You can visit him at kencraftpoetry.wordpress.com.

www.ingramcontent.com/pod-product-compliance
Lightning Source LLC
Chambersburg PA
CBHW071100090426
42737CB00013B/2399